SOURCES
AI
DELIVERY
AF584454

FANTASTIC FACTS ABOUT

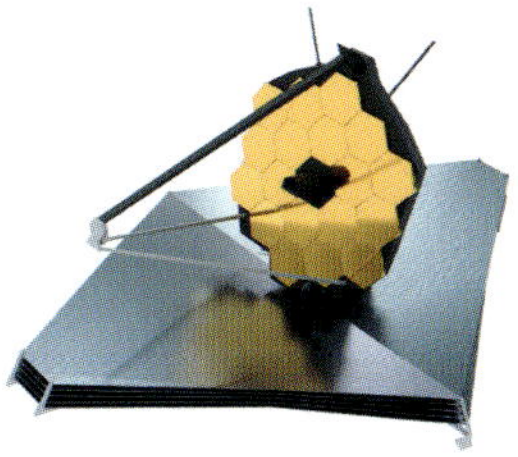

AI ARTIFICIAL INTELLIGENCE

WARREN SINGER

REDBACK publishing

First Published 2025 by
Redback Publishing
Suite 6, 13a Narabang Way,
Belrose NSW 2085
Australia

www.redbackpublishing.com
info@redbackpublishing.com

ISBN 978-1-761401-24-4

Author: Warren Singer
Editor: Caroline Thomas
Designer: Redback Publishing

Original illustrations © Redback Publishing 2025
Originated by Redback Publishing

Acknowledgements
Abbreviations: l—left, r—right, b—bottom, t—top, c—centre, m—middle
We would like to thank the following for permission to reproduce photographs: (Images © shutterstock),
p11mr Boumen Japet/Shutterstock.com, p12tl Mojahid Mottakin/Shutterstock.com, p13br AlesiaKan/Shutterstock.com, p20tr NASA/IPI-Caltech Public domain via Wikimedia Commons, p23mr Diego Thomazini/Shutterstock.com, p27bl Ververidis Vasilis/Shutterstock.com

A catalogue record for this book is available from the National Library of Australia

CONTENTS

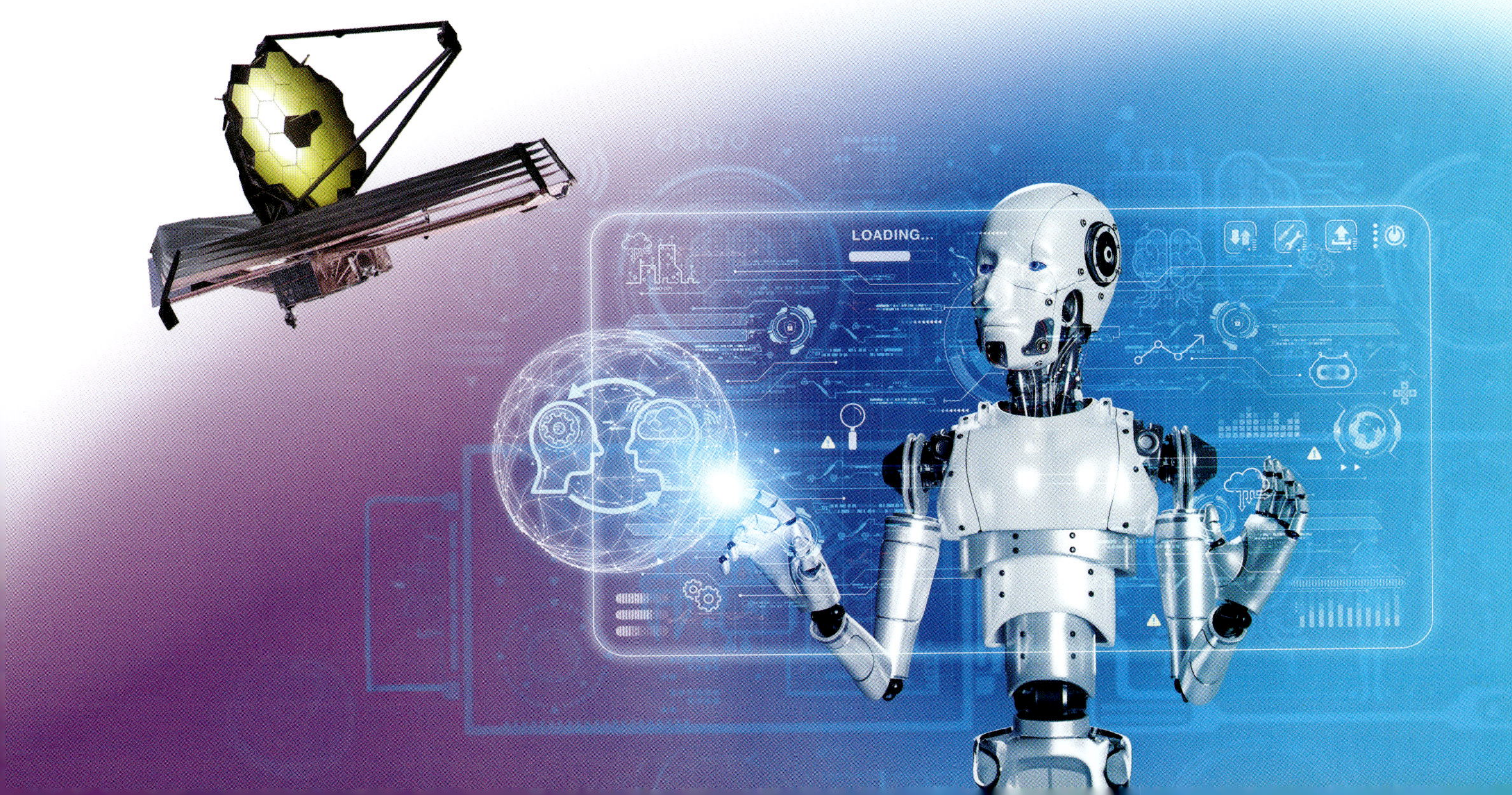

Quick Facts

These quick facts will get you started on your quest to find out all you want to know about AI (artificial intelligence).

WHAT IS AI?

AI involves the use of computer algorithms to complete tasks in a more efficient way than humans could otherwise do themselves.

HOW OLD IS AI?

AI has been a serious field of scientific study since the middle of the last century.

WILL AI MAKE LIFE EASIER FOR US ALL?

It's possible, but the future of the interactions between AI and humans is not yet known for certain.

DOES AI KNOW WHAT WE ARE THINKING?

AI uses the data we give it to calculate what we might be thinking.

IS AI ALIVE?

No, it is not alive, but it may appear to have a sort of machine consciousness.

WILL AI BE EQUALLY AVAILABLE TO EVERYONE IN THE WORLD?

Since nothing is equally available at present to everyone, it is unlikely that the situation will change for AI.

WILL AI DESTROY HUMANITY IF WE TRY TO SHUT IT DOWN?

That all depends on the way AI has been created by humans, and the data and power they have allowed it to use.

Artificial Intelligence

WHAT IS ARTIFICIAL INTELLIGENCE?

Living things have intelligence, ranging from simple to complex. Worms know to move away from sunlight while humans can use complex mathematics or create beautiful artworks. These are both forms of living intelligence. When a computer runs software to produce outcomes, without a human having to tell it what to do at every step, then this is artificial intelligence.

TYPES OF AI

The main types of AI are:

GENERATIVE AI - can create new text, images, videos and audio files based on information from other databases that it has been given access to.

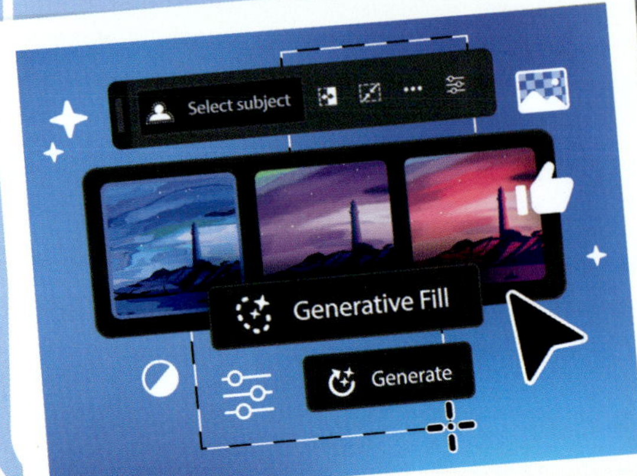

TRADITIONAL AI - does not create anything new, but uses the data it is given to present things like sales reports, or to do tasks such as telling a robot where to put the rivets in a car that it is making.

WEAK OR STRONG AI?

As with any new field of science, the words used to describe what is being discovered and invented are changing quickly. The terms weak AI and strong AI are just two examples.

WEAK AI - AI that is not able to behave as though it is thinking like a human.

STRONG AI - AI that appears to have consciousness and an awareness of what is going on around it.

AGI

AGI, artificial general intelligence, is the AI of the future. AGI may surpass all the capabilities of AI because it can do more than just calculate based on previous programming created by humans. AGI may be able to alter its own programming, making the possible outcomes both spectacular and terrifying.

Can AI Think?

HUMAN VS COMPUTER

Human thinking involves using all of the past experiences stored in our brains to come up with a thought that is relevant to the present. In the same way, a computer uses coded software to interpret information from the databases that it has been given access to.

ALGORITHMS

An algorithm is a set of coding instructions that tell a computer what to do. AI starts with a set of algorithms that a human software engineer has written. If this code has instructions in it that allow the program to create its own algorithms, then the AI could progress far beyond the original instructions.

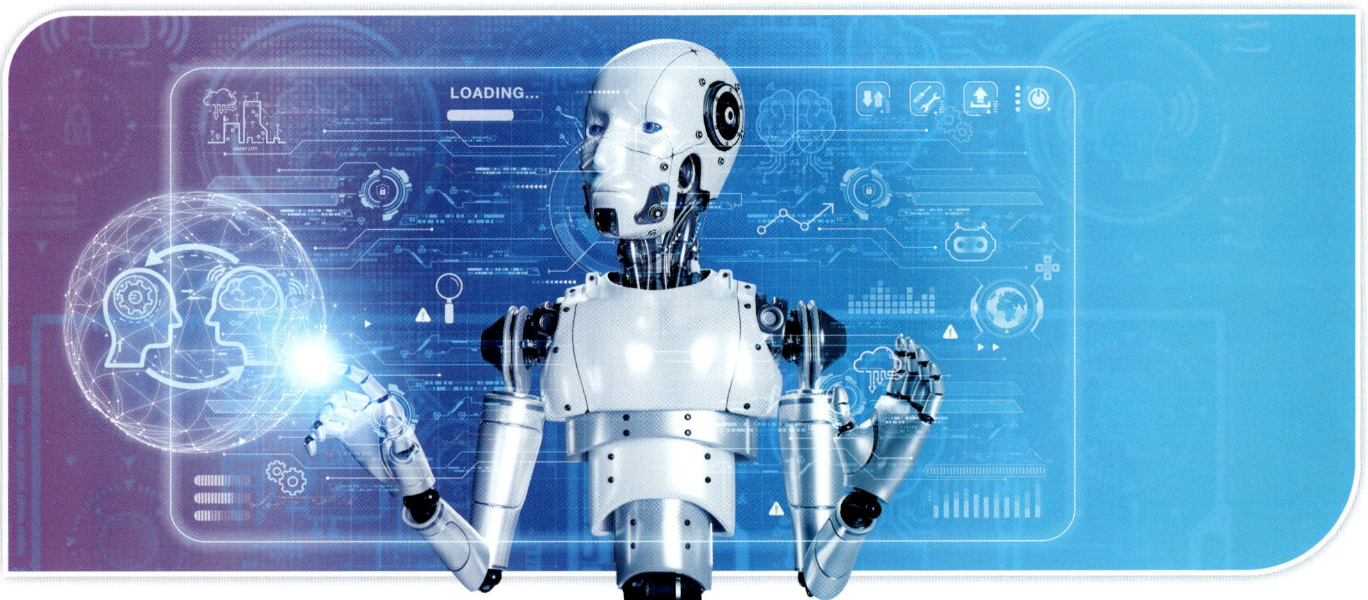

CAN AI THINK?

Whether a machine can ever think is a serious philosophical question. Machines can certainly appear to think, and many of us have been fooled into believing that a computer-generated voice might be a real person.

However, the concept of 'real' thought is debated by both scientists and philosophers, since the power to 'think', in both cases, is simply a matter of electrical impulse. Who is to say that carbon (the building block of humans) is a more effective or sustainable basis for 'thought' or reasoning than silicon (the building block of AI)?

DEEP NEURAL NETWORKS

DNN, deep neural network, is a type of algorithm used in the building of AI. It enables software to do tasks such as image recognition based on huge amounts of data, and other jobs that are beyond the capabilities of humans.

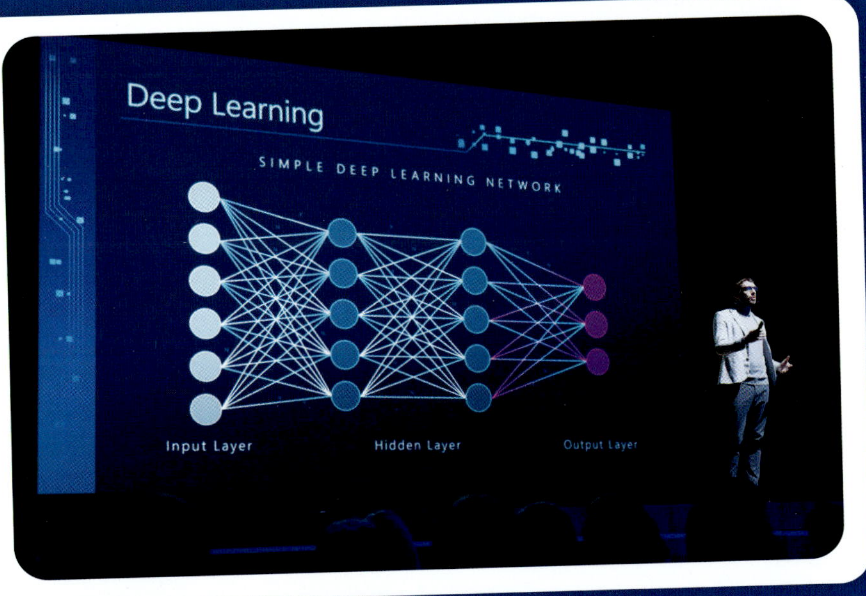

Who Uses AI?

MOST OF US ALREADY USE AI

There are many examples of AI in everyday life, including:

- Playing online games such as chess
- Using an Internet search engine
- Riding in a car with lights that turn on automatically when needed
- Talking to a computer-generated voice on the phone
- Having a multiple-choice test checked by a computer instead of a teacher

BUSINESS

AI has been used in factories, businesses and on farms for decades. For many years, AI robots have been making cars, and computer software has been used to calculate and pay a company's taxes. Recent advances in AI have allowed it to go even further than this. AI can now predict what will happen and make its own changes to what it should do in light of those predictions.

WHAT COULD GO WRONG?

Humans programmed the software that now powers AI. The programming is so complex and interconnected, that the outcomes can be unexpected. For example, a machine that relies on AI to put parts together in a factory, can mistake a nearby human arm for a piece it needs to grab, with disastrous results.

AI GENERATED WORDS AND IMAGES

AI programs are increasing in number and usability. They can now write essays, do your homework, answer medical and legal questions, and even create new images that have never existed before. This is all done based on algorithms or coding. The program learns more about what its future users will want each time it answers a query or produces an image. The more that people use it, the better it will become in the quality of its outputs.

AI and Truth

WHAT IS THE TRUTH?

An AI word and image production program that is Internet-based cannot tell us if an essay it writes for us is truthful. It can only determine that the information it included in that essay has appeared in many sites on the Internet. AI that quotes its sources is therefore preferable to use, since we can then see where the information has come from and determine if the sources can be believed.

GETTING IT WRONG

Internet-based AI word and image production programs can give you answers that are not exactly untruthful, but that are still wrong. If you ask for information and are not specific enough in your words, AI may return an answer that refers to something that is not about the topic you wanted. If you are not sure yourself about the subject you want AI to research, then you may not even realise that the information it has given you is wrong.

HALLUCINATION

In the AI world, a wrong response, such as presenting you with an essay on a living bat, when what you wanted was information on a cricket bat, is called an hallucination.

TRANSPARENCY

Transparent use of AI means that a person who has used AI to generate an item, such as text, image, audio or video, makes this very clear and does not present the output as though it is entirely their own work. Transparency also means that any person or business using AI to conduct a conversation, or make decisions about what happens to people who are customers or clients, makes it clear that AI is involved.

AI and Copying

AI AND COPYRIGHT

Copyright is the right of artists, writers and other creative people to have ownership of their work. Copyright laws exist in most countries to protect the rights of these people. Work that appears on the Internet is usually covered by copyright law and cannot be used or copied without permission. When using AI to write about a topic or create an image, be aware that the program is accessing other people's work. If you then present that work as your own, this could cause copyright problems.

KEEPING UP

Legal and other regulation of AI has not kept up with the advances in technology. People using AI products need to find out for themselves if the words they are presenting as their own are actually copied from someone else's work. An Internet search usually shows the source of the information, but if you ask an AI program to find this for you, it may not reveal its sources.

AI AND PLAGIARISM

Plagiarism is something most school students learn about as soon as they start writing and researching for themselves. It refers to the use of the work of another person as though it is your own. Since Internet-based AI word and image programs search the web for information to complete whatever request you have made, they are using other people's work as their sources. If you then claim that this work is your own, you could be guilty of plagiarism.

AI Helps Us

VIRTUAL HELPERS

AI has some very useful roles to play in assisting people. Virtual assistants can talk to lonely people, help those who are visually challenged, assist with contacting human helpers, provide training courses, and generally assist with everyday tasks.

AI is also being used to help people with artificial limbs to use them more effectively. AI does this by using data from nerve signals and applying this to the movement of the artificial hand, arm, leg or foot.

CHATBOTS

Chatbots are software applications that produce answers to questions made either online or on a telephone call. In the simplest chatbots, the application listens or looks for keywords in a question to tell it what sort of stored answer to present to the customer. This is why you will sometimes get an answer that is constantly repeated or is not relevant to your complete question. Siri, Google Assistant and Alexa are examples of more complex, conversational chatbots.

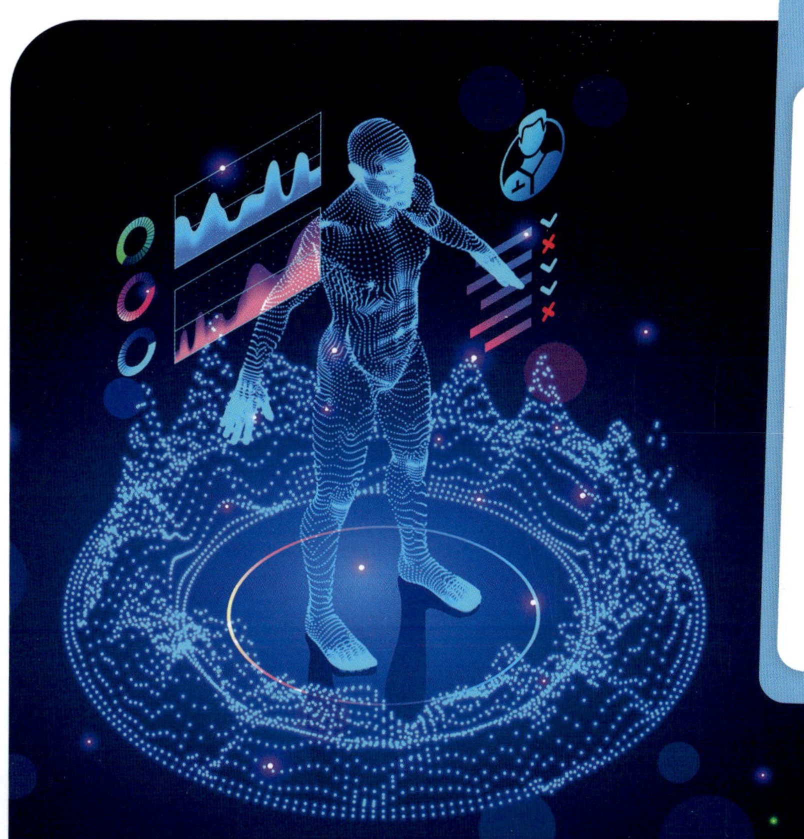

AI IN MEDICINE

AI can be trained to diagnose illnesses, keep track of the vital signs of a patient, respond if something life-threatening occurs, read the results of patients' tests and determine if anything looks unusual. Unlike humans, who make mistakes when they are tired or overworked, AI can do its tasks 24 hours a day without resting. This can lead to good results for patients, as long as errors in algorithms, or other failures in function, do not occur. The results of such failures could be fatal.

AI AND HUMANOID ROBOTS

In the past, people used to imagine that interaction with humanoid robots would be the way that we used AI in our daily lives, but this is not the way the new AI technology has developed. Although some humanoid robots exist, the majority of the AI we encounter is delivered to us through computers with which we interact. Rather than talking to a robot that looks like a metal person in our home, we talk to a digital assistant, our computer or a chatbot on a phone.

AI in War

AI IN BATTLE

AI is used by military organisations around the world to assess the dangers of wartime situations. For example, AI can suggest when and where to strike at the enemy, and it can guide unmanned vehicles.

CRITICS

Critics of AI have suggested that allowing it to make military decisions could lead to dangerous situations that might make wartime conditions worse. The possibility of placing AI software in charge of using destructive weapons is something that could result in unwanted consequences.

WARTIME SPYING

Spying has been a part of warfare for thousands of years. It used to depend on human spies finding out what the enemy was up to. With AI systems in use, a nation at war can survey vast areas from satellites or drones and pick out objects of interest. These might include build-ups of military vehicles, or clearing of large spaces where weapons might be installed.

SPYING ON COMMUNICATIONS

The massive amount of communication that happens all around the world is too vast for humans to monitor in detail. An AI system can do this quickly and efficiently, picking up word patterns that could suggest an enemy's wartime plans.

AI in Space

JAMES WEBB SPACE TELESCOPE

The James Webb Space Telescope, launched by NASA in 2021, has returned data about billions of objects in the far reaches of outer space. Human analysis of all this data is impossible, so scientists use the AI system called Morpheus to do it instead. It can analyse every pixel of the images sent back to Earth.

Images created from data supllied by the James Webb Telesope.

The Mars Perseverance Rover descended to the planet's surface via a parachute.

MARS ROVER

In 2022, NASA's Mars Rover began using AI to help it decide which rocks to study in its search for the remnants of life on the red planet. Since instructions from scientists on Earth take so long to get to the Rover, it can use AI to make its own choices without having to wait for a person to tell it what to do.

AI at School

USING AI ETHICALLY

GPT usage is now so widespread, that banning it is not possible. Instead, students are being encouraged to learn how to use it ethically. The more they know about AI, the better they will be able to spot fake content presented as real by others.

AI FOR DISADVANTAGED STUDENTS

AI has the potential to improve the education of students in places where they are disadvantaged through having few resources and a lack of trained teachers. AI can help to track the learning of students and give them personalised hints on what they need to do to advance in their education.

GPT GENERATIVE PRE-TRAINED TRANSFORMER

When GPT-based AI started appearing everywhere in the early 2020s, the first thought at many schools and universities was that it should be banned. Teachers thought that if students students used GPT technology to write essays, it would be almost impossible to tell if the content was their own work or that of AI. As newer versions of GPT were created, the quality of the output became even better, and is now almost at a point where it can match the output produced by an average human.

PRIVACY AT SCHOOL

When schools rely on AI to help teach their students, there is the possibility that unwanted access to student data can occur. Learning about the importance of privacy when interacting with AI will be as important as learning about the subject that students are studying.

AI Problems

FALSE NEWS AND AI

People searching for something interesting to read on the Internet are naturally drawn to outrageous stories that are probably not true. AI systems can track your Internet use to learn more about what you like. AI then uses this information to show you more of what it thinks you might like to see. This creates a very narrow view of the world and can result in a bias towards conspiracy theories, fake news and in serious cases, dangerous radical ideas becoming accepted as normal. In this way, some people can develop the belief that all outrageous information must be true, since it forms so much of what they see online.

KEYWORD CHECK

It is important to always be aware that your top results from an Internet search may be based on AI's decisions about what it thinks you want to see and may not reflect what the real-world situation is.

Try searching the same keywords on a friend's device, and see for yourself how different the results can be!

AI AND PREJUDICE

The algorithms that tell AI what to look for when deciding if a group of people are a danger to society or not have been found to sometimes show bias and prejudice, even when the original software engineer did not do this on purpose.

PREJUDICE

Using large sets of data that have been obtained from many sources may produce prejudiced results. For example, AI might look at the home suburb of a person in question, and see the suburb has a high level of people with criminal convictions. AI might then decide that the person being checked is also a threat. This decision may not reflect the actual individual's character and can result in unfair discrimination.

AI and Loss of Jobs

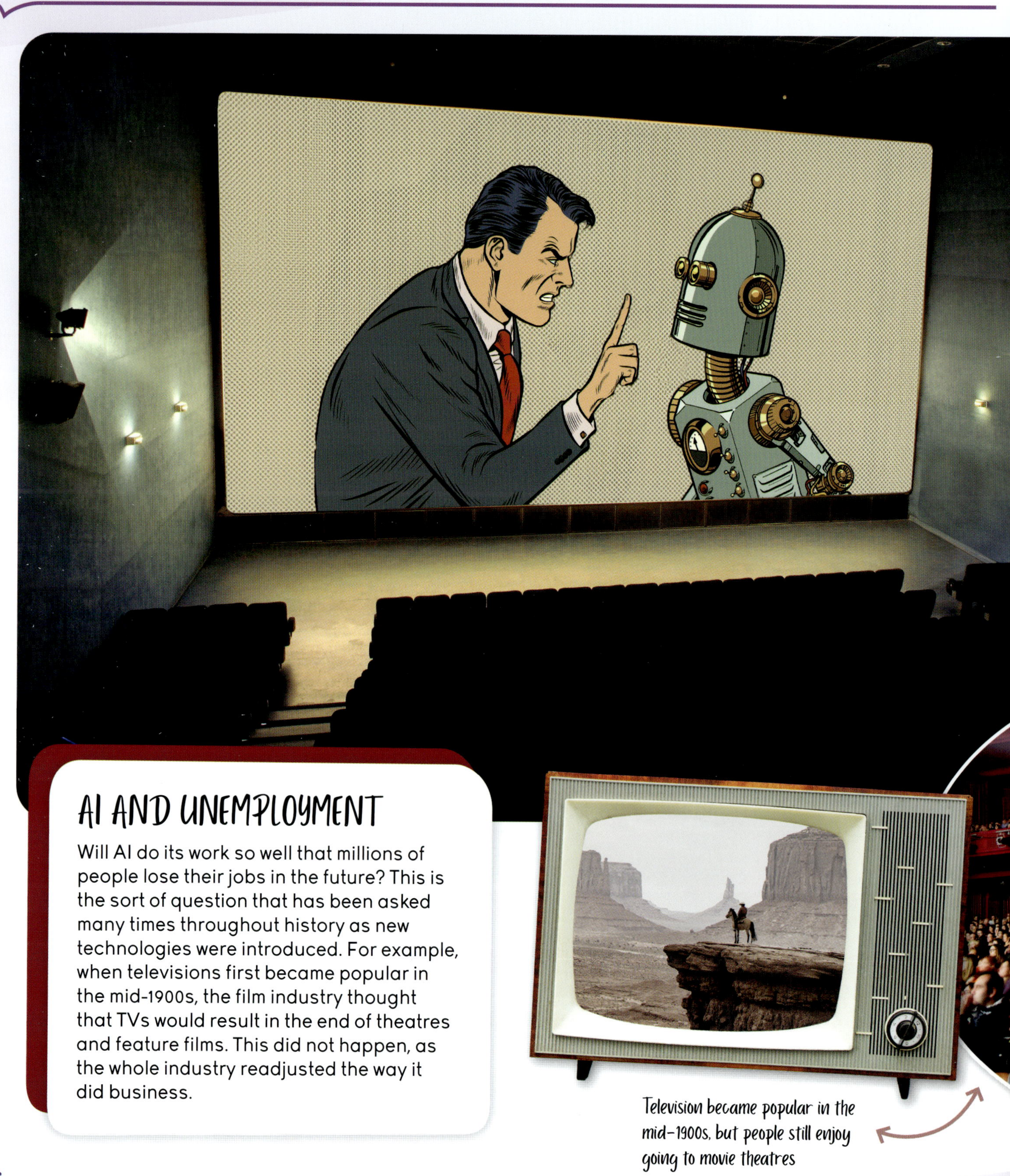

AI AND UNEMPLOYMENT

Will AI do its work so well that millions of people lose their jobs in the future? This is the sort of question that has been asked many times throughout history as new technologies were introduced. For example, when televisions first became popular in the mid-1900s, the film industry thought that TVs would result in the end of theatres and feature films. This did not happen, as the whole industry readjusted the way it did business.

Television became popular in the mid-1900s, but people still enjoy going to movie theatres

JOBS ST RISK?

The jobs that might be lost in the future due to AI include data entry operators, bookkeepers, accountants and sales assistants in shops.

LUDDITES

A person who refuses to believe that new technology can be worthwhile is called a Luddite. Luddites were people in the early 1800s who lost their jobs as weavers when machinery replaced them. They wanted to keep their jobs and formed gangs that destroyed the new machines.

The introduction of new technology has always resulted in the loss of some jobs and the creation of new ones, but this process does take time.

Keeping AI Under Control

LEGAL CONTROL

AI is advancing so quickly, that law making bodies cannot keep up. There is worldwide discussion about controlling the use of AI with laws, but even if these are passed by world governments, there will always be some countries that will not comply.

REPLACING US

The earliest generative AI was so clumsy and full of errors that most people thought it would never replace human beings. They decided that legislation to control it was not a matter of urgency, but ongoing advances have proven that decision to be wrong.

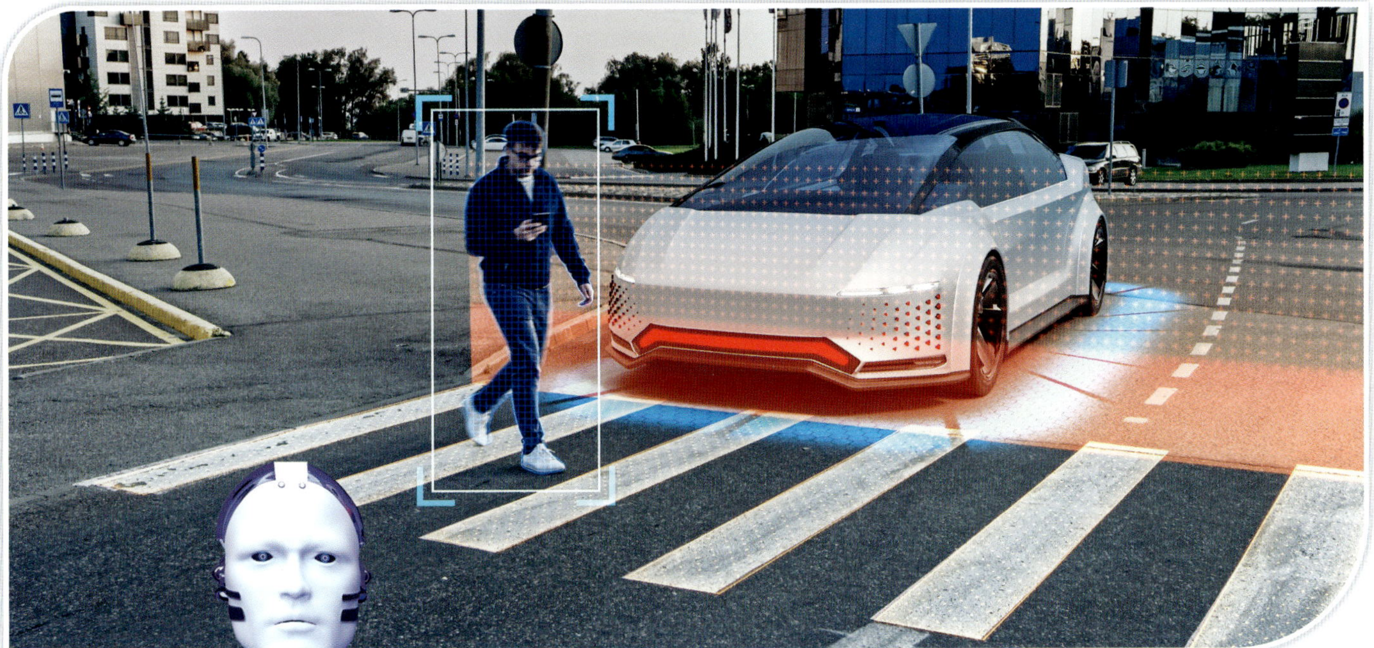

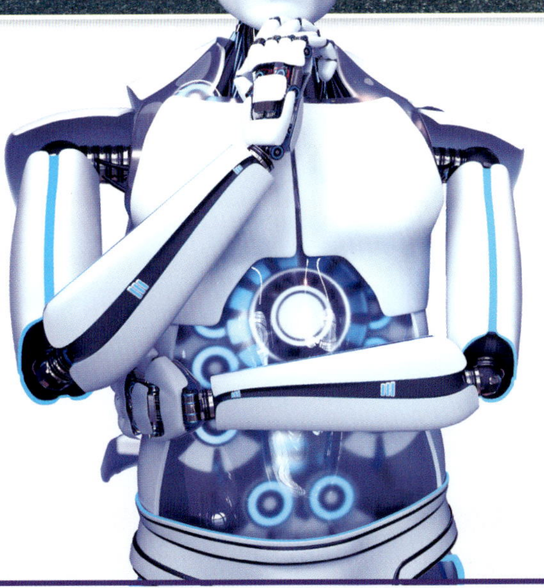

RIGHT AND WRONG

All human societies produce ideals for what is right and wrong. Human intelligence operates daily based on these ideals. How will AGI deal with right and wrong and create outcomes that are not harmful to life? Even now, the logic that the AI in a self-driving car has to use, forces it to decide in an accident situation whether to take an action that will either save the driver or a person who walks out in front of the moving car. This same sort of decision making, if left to AGI without further human intervention, could yield unexpected results in every field where AGI is in control of what happens.

CONSCIOUSNESS

Is consciousness just a series of pathways in the brain, or is a soul involved? Can a machine ever be conscious? If it can, then would a human be killing the machine by switching it off or destroying its parts?

AI, Past and Future

FUTURE AI

We are on the verge of an AI revolution that will alter the way we interact with each other, learn and do business. The possibilities are exciting, but controlling the changes to come are challenges that we will need to face and manage.

Some people think we should stop all AI development now and not continue until we know more about the possible adverse effects of what is being produced. Others believe that human invention should never be stifled, and that we should deal with consequences as they occur.

Glossary

collision	when objects smash into each other
AGI	artificial general intelligence
algorithm	coding that tells a computer what to do
chatbot	computer-generated voice or text that answers queries
complex	complicated
consciousness	being aware of oneself
copyright	right of a creative person to own their output
DNN	deep neural network: method used by AI to process large amounts of data
ethically	with regard to what is right and wrong
GPT	generative pre-trained transformer: used to create text or images
hallucination	wrong or untruthful response generated by GPT
philosophy	study of knowledge and existence
plagiarism	using someone else's creative work without acknowledgement
predict	guess what will happen in the future
rivet	small metal rod used for joining things
stifle	stop something happening
vital signs	in health care, the signs of life such as heartbeat and blood pressure

Index

SOURCES
AI
DELIVERY